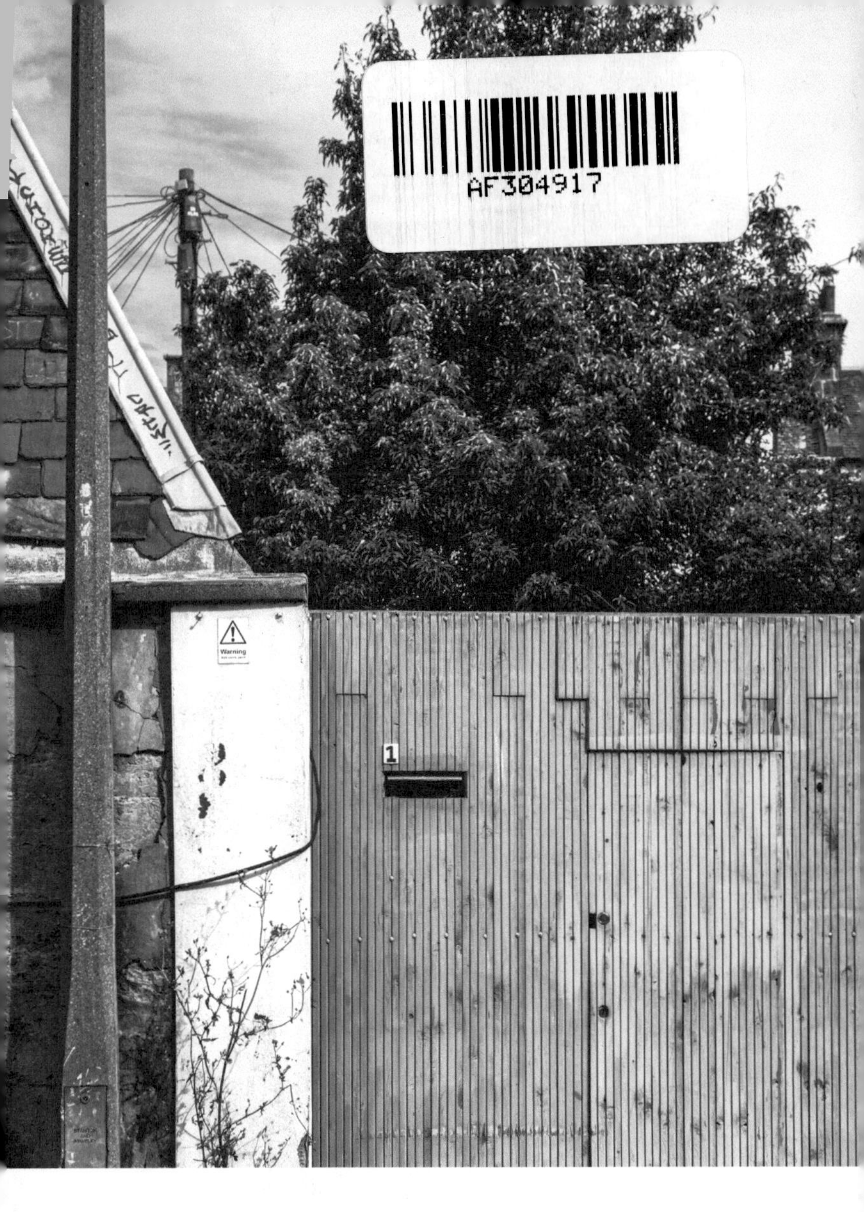

WE HAVE SUBDUED THE FORCES OF NATURE

AND PRESSED THEM INTO THE SERVICE OF MANKIND

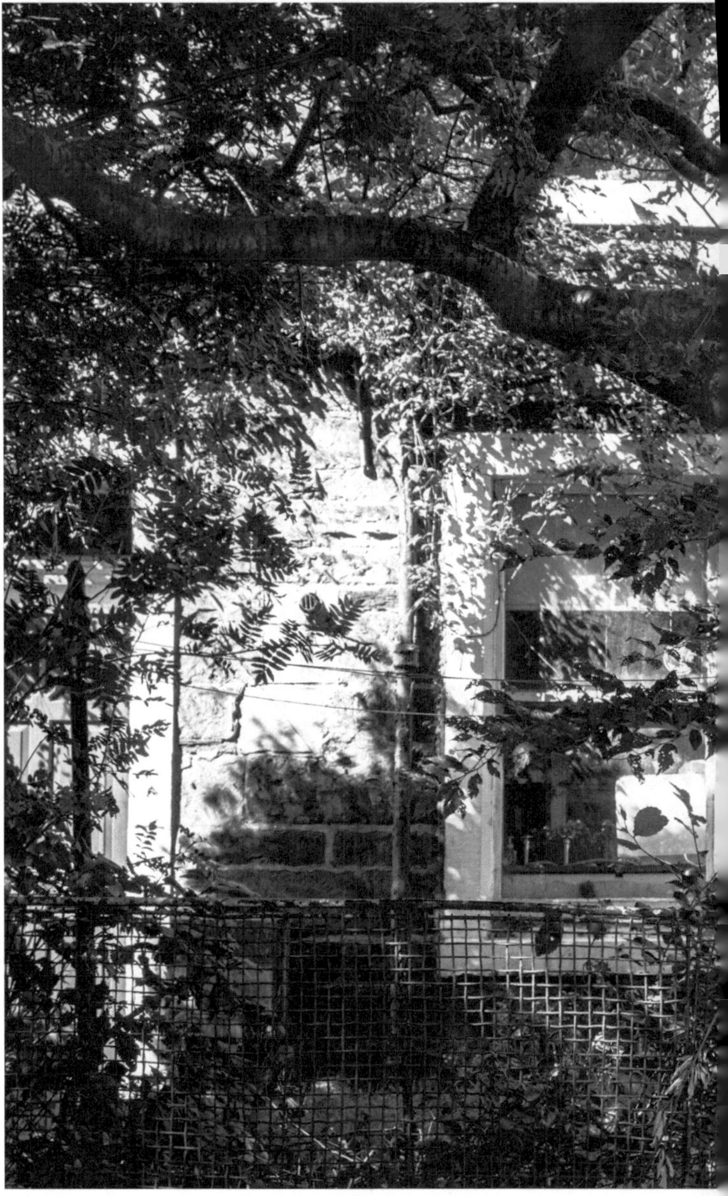

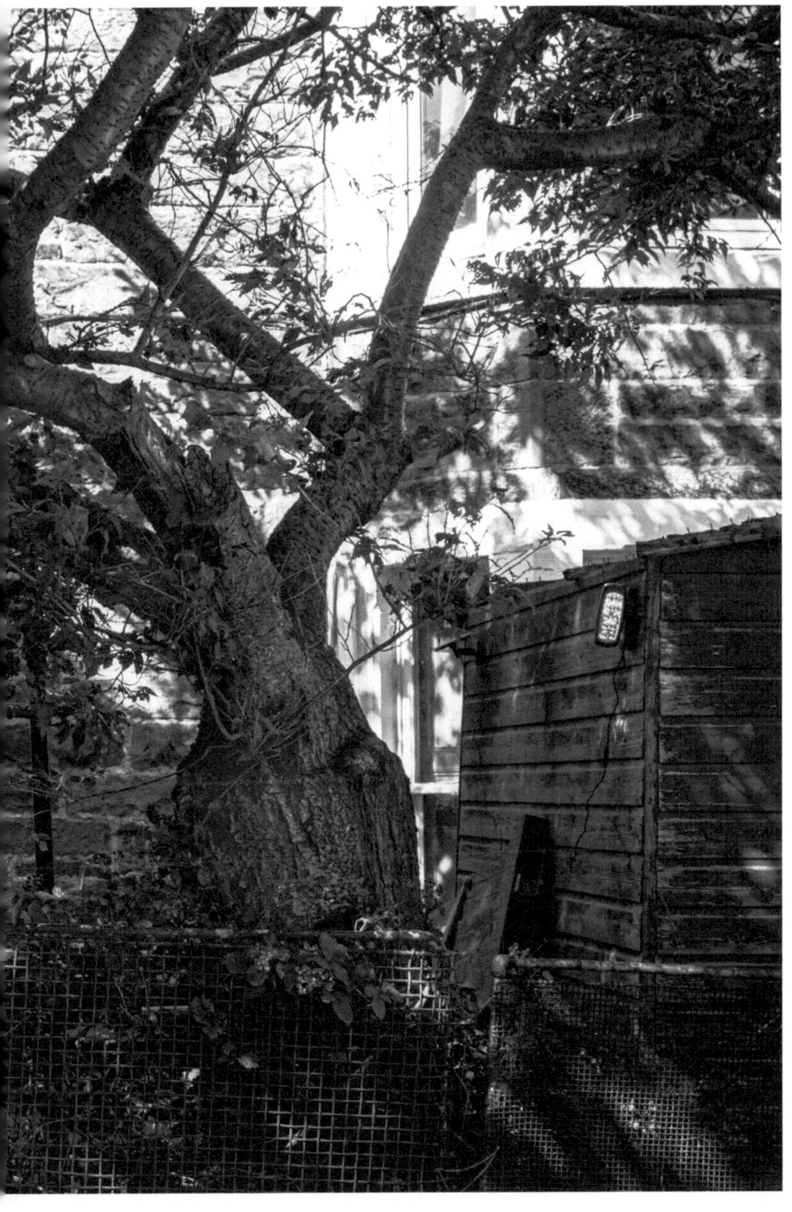

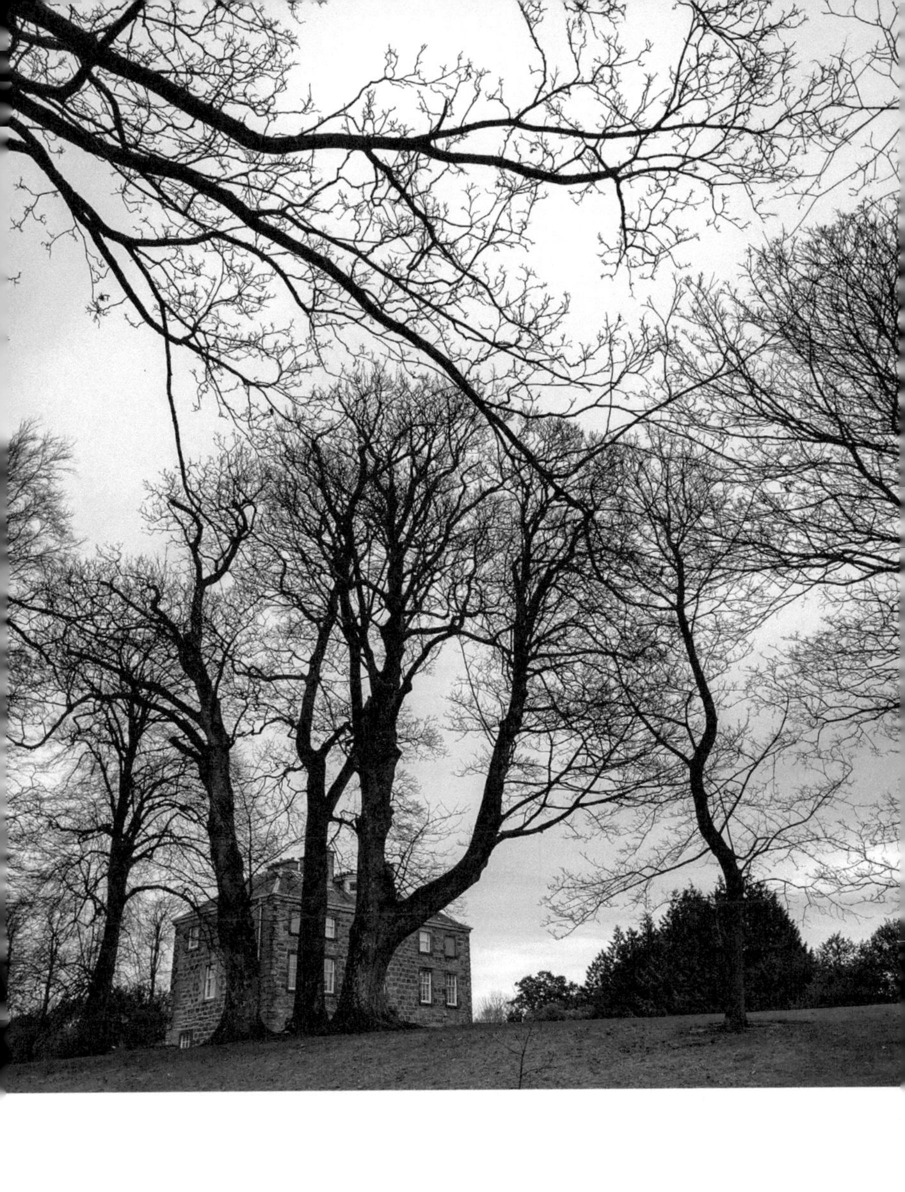

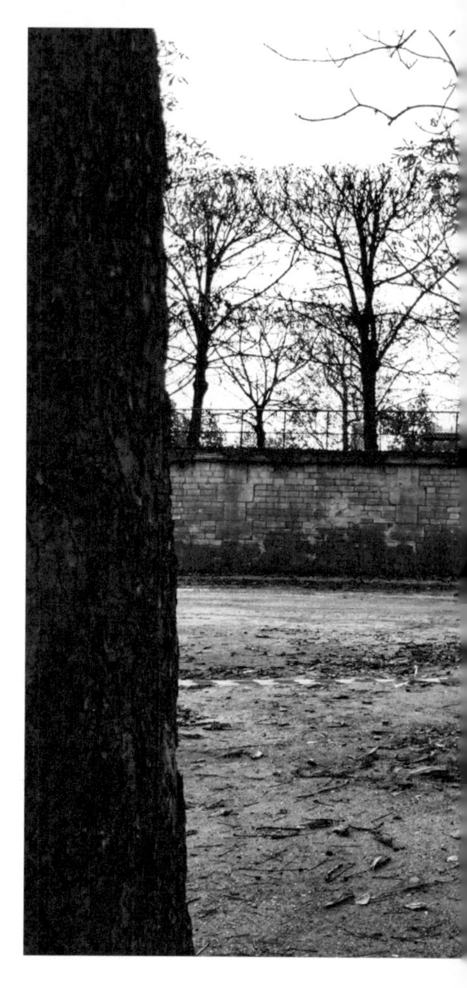

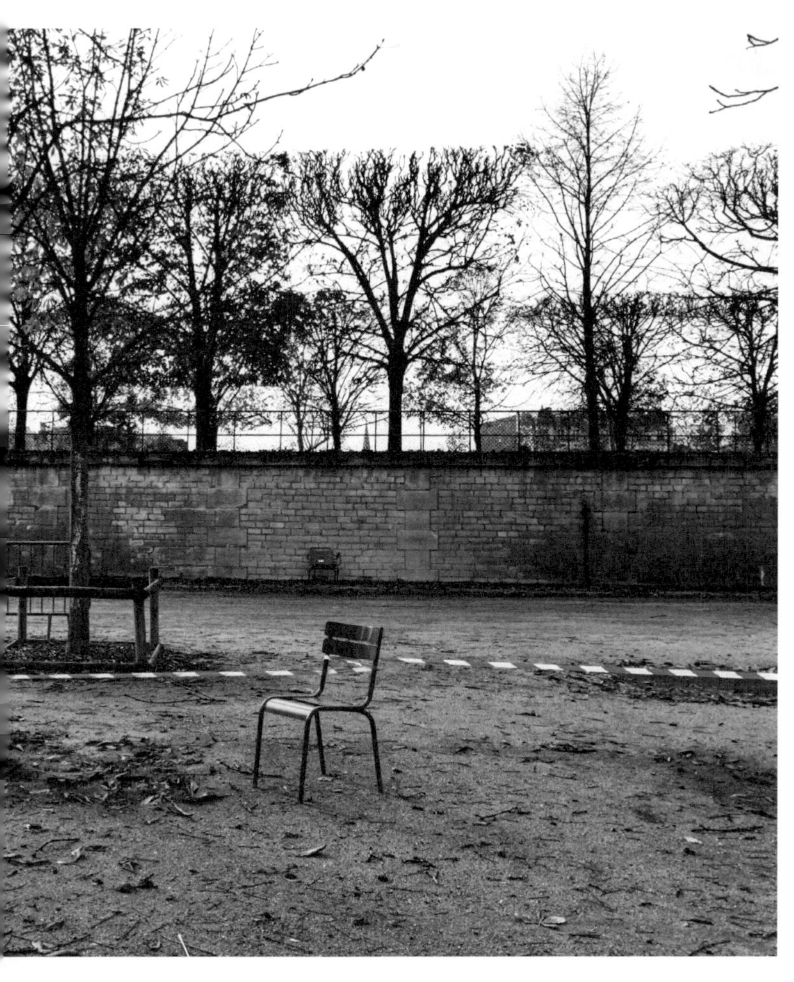

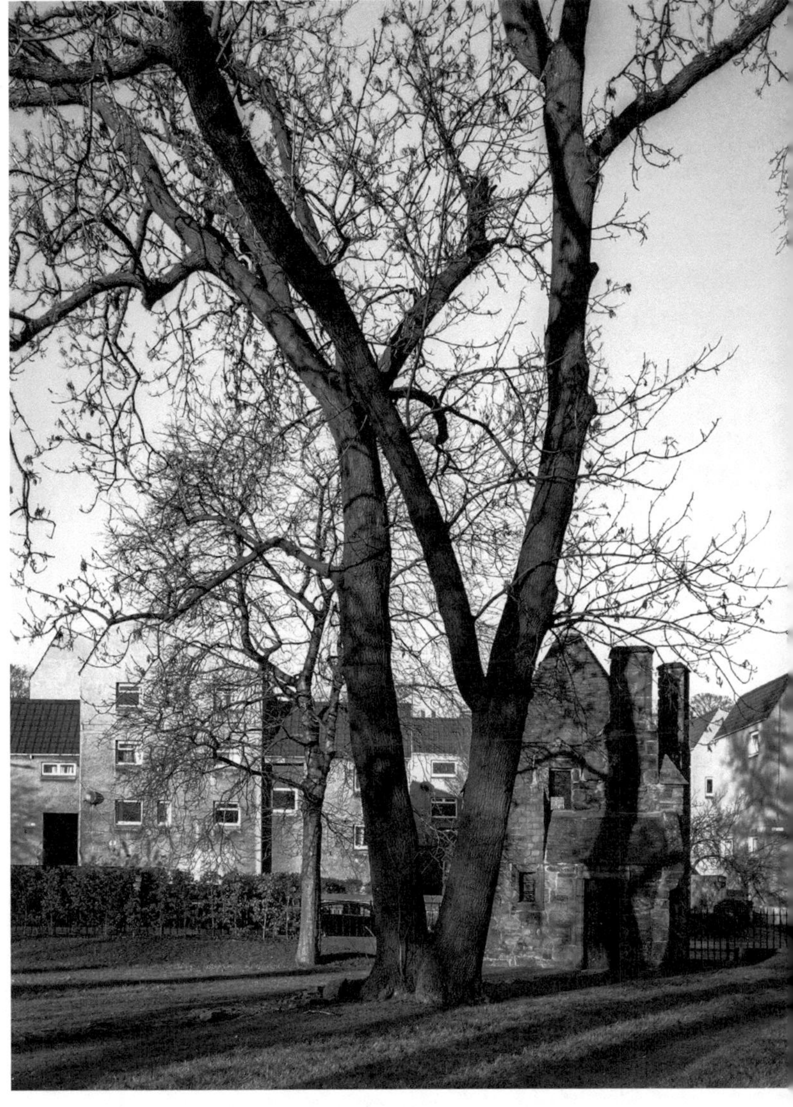

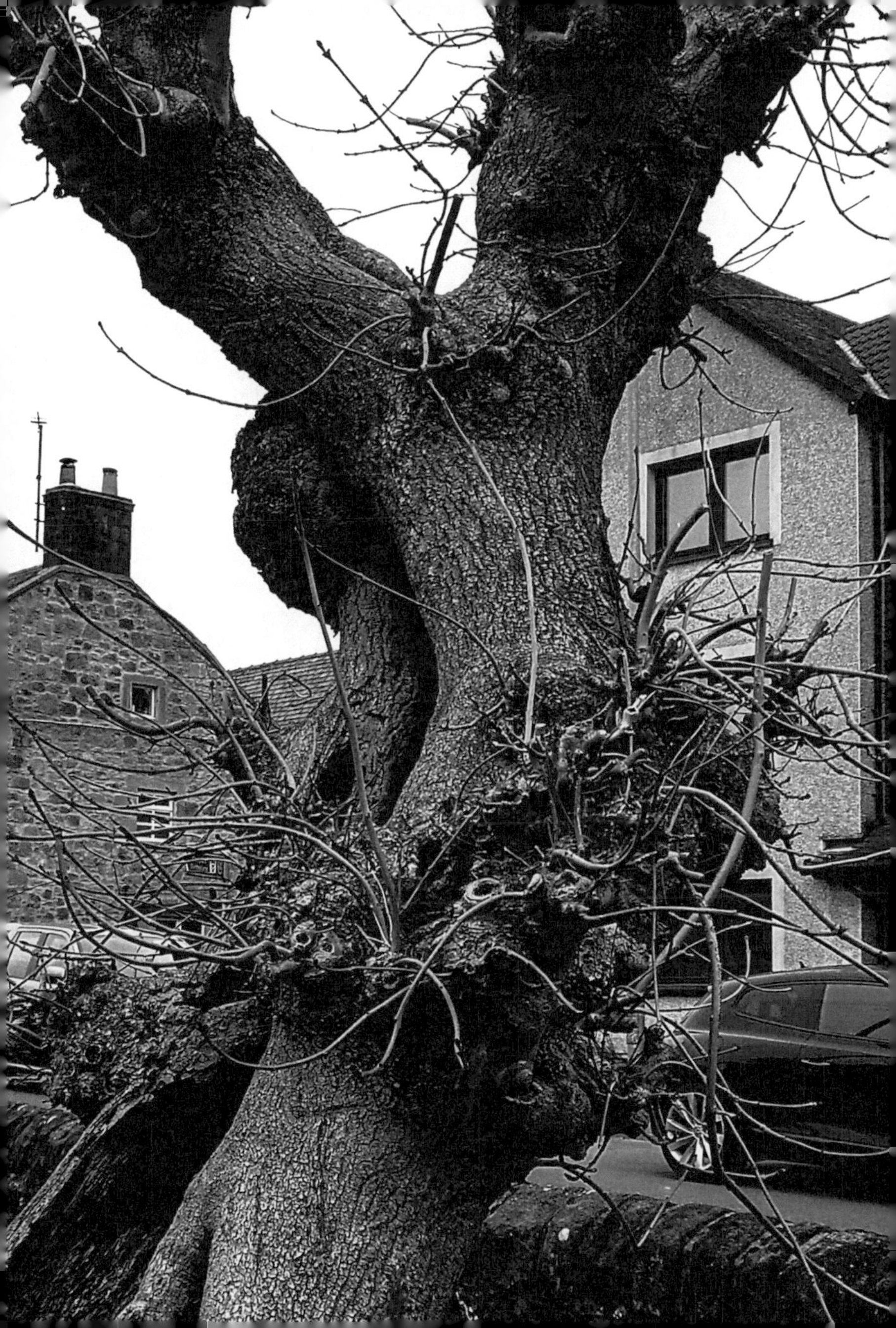

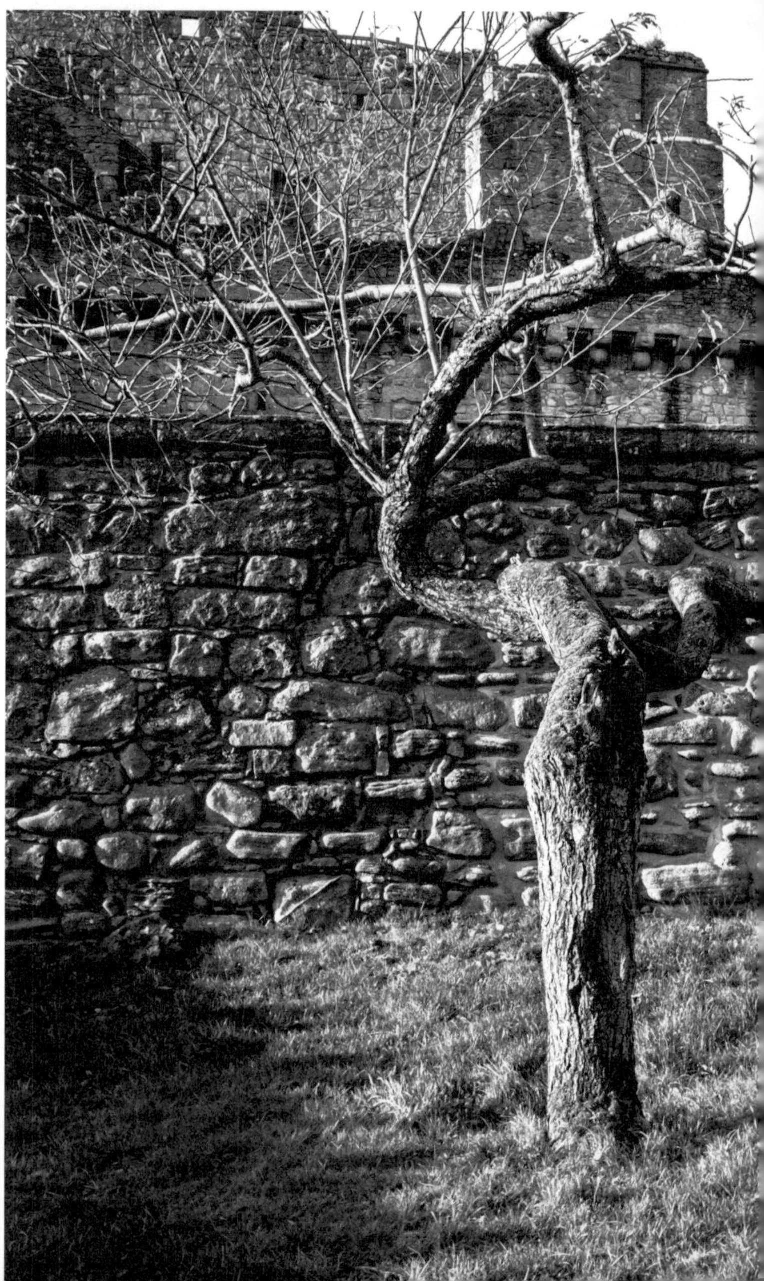

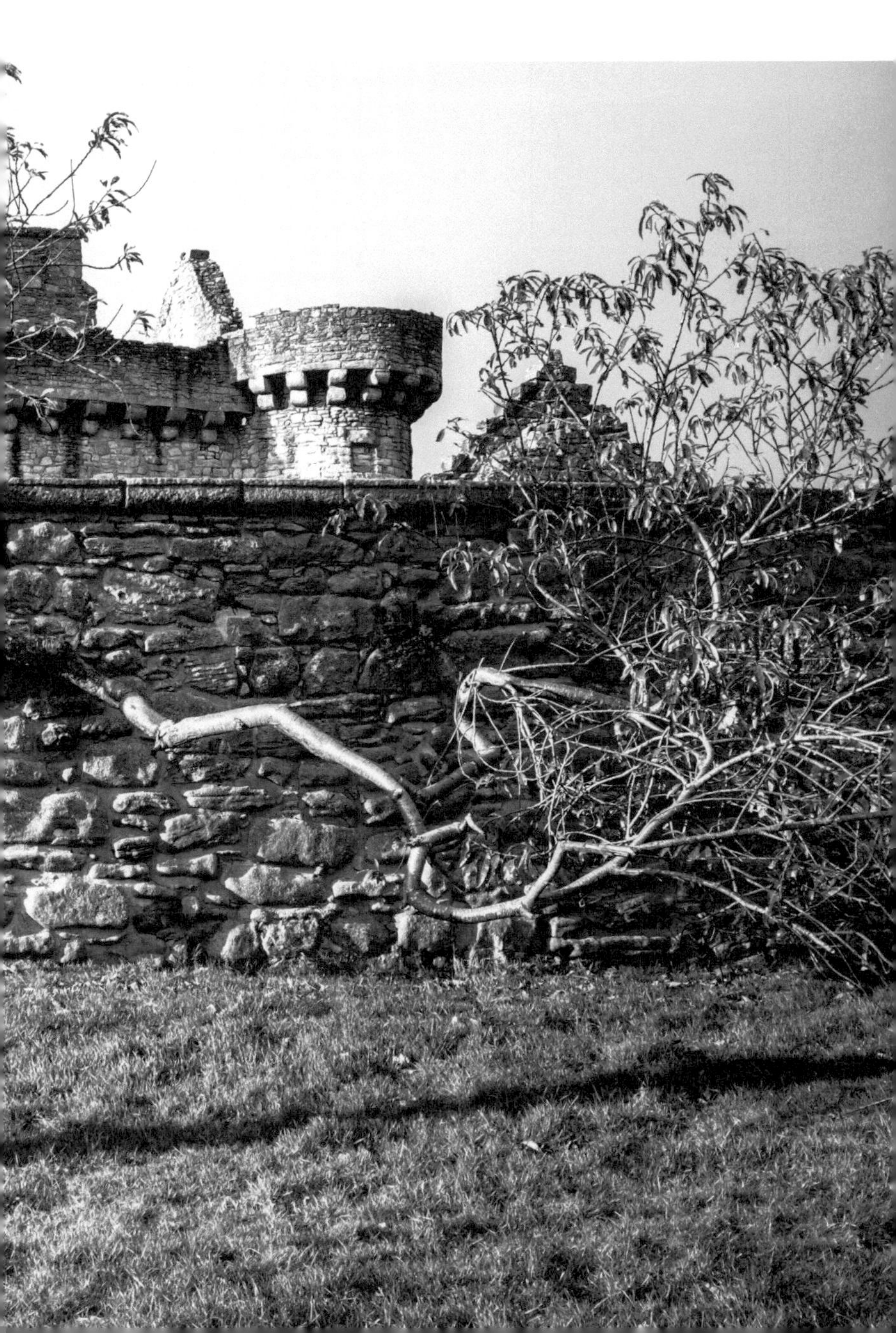

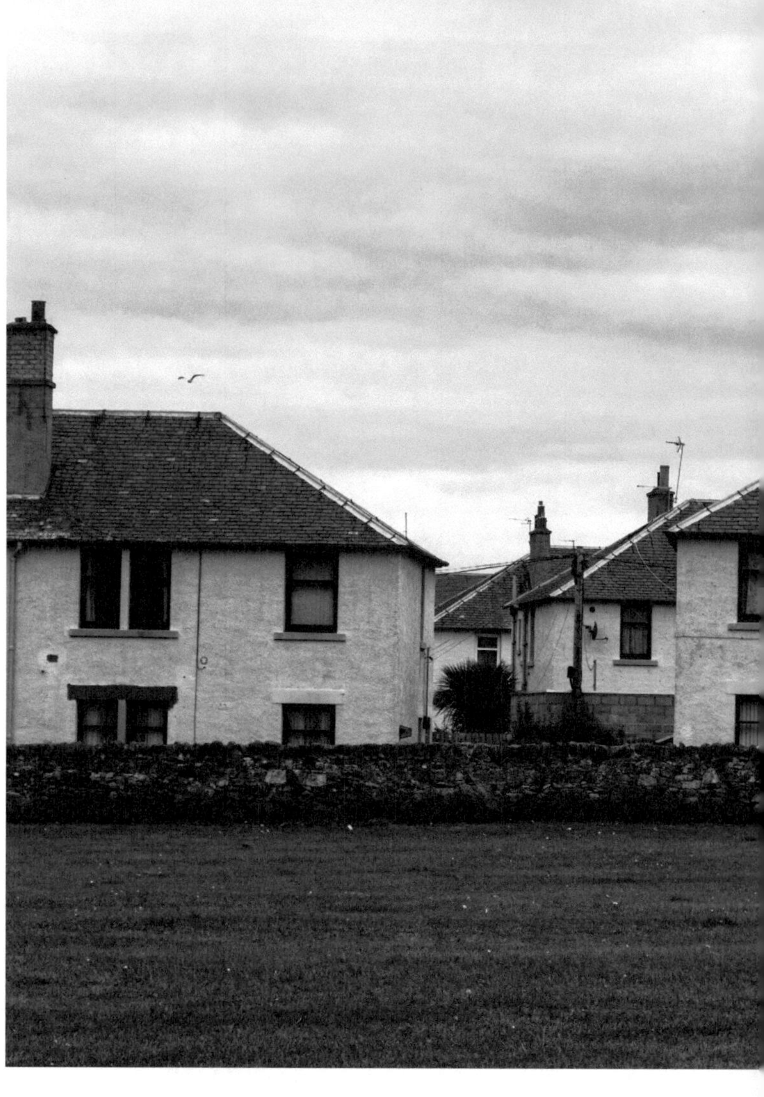

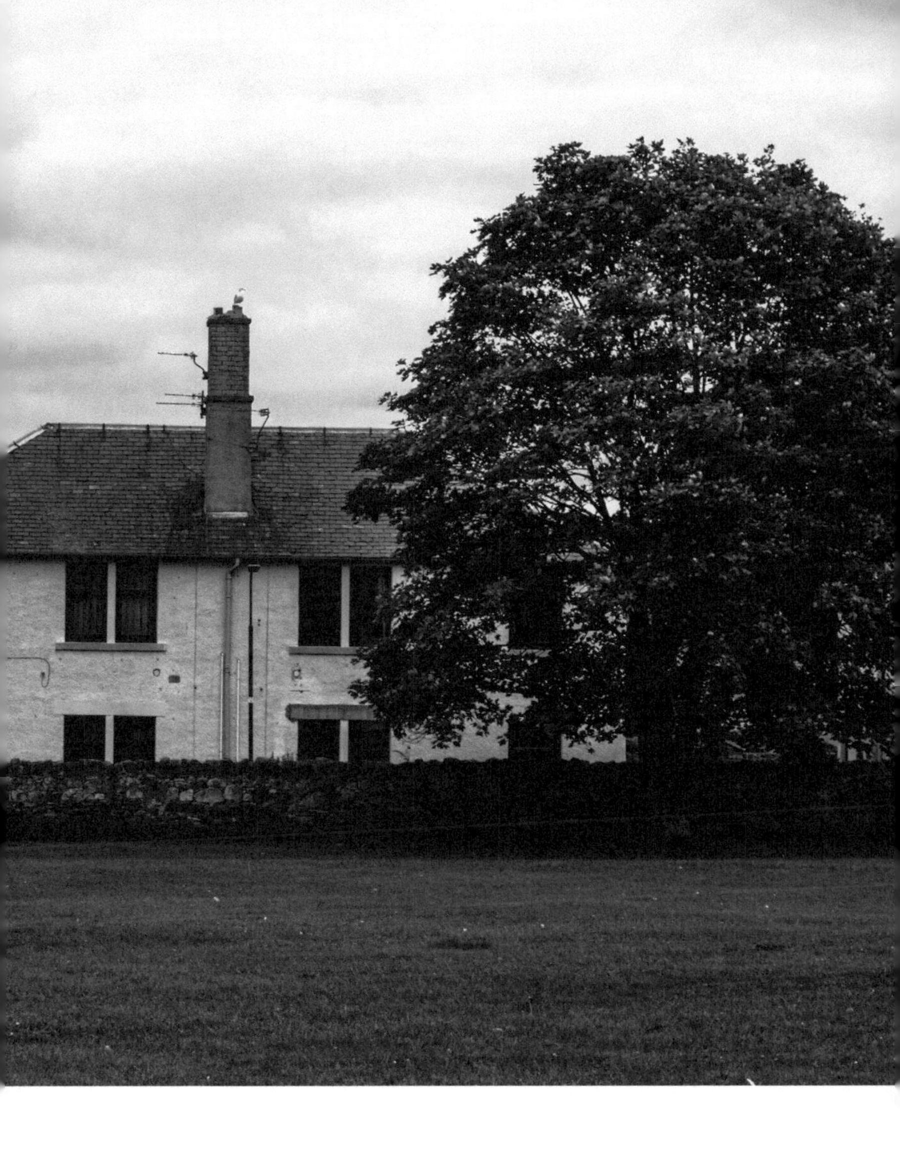

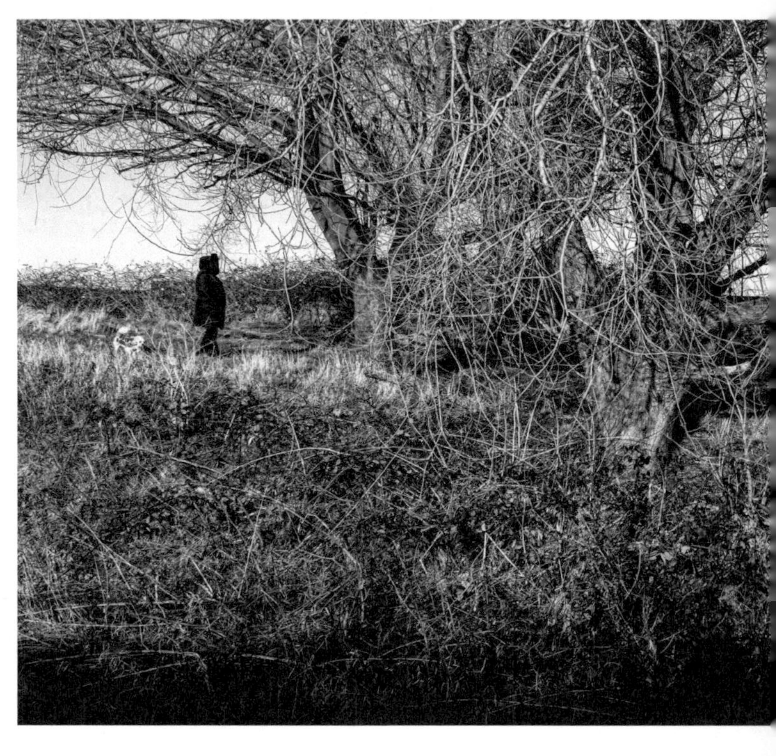

AND WHAT IS THE RESULT?
INCREASING OVERWORK AND MISERY OF THE MASSES
AND EVERY TEN YEARS A GREAT COLLAPSE

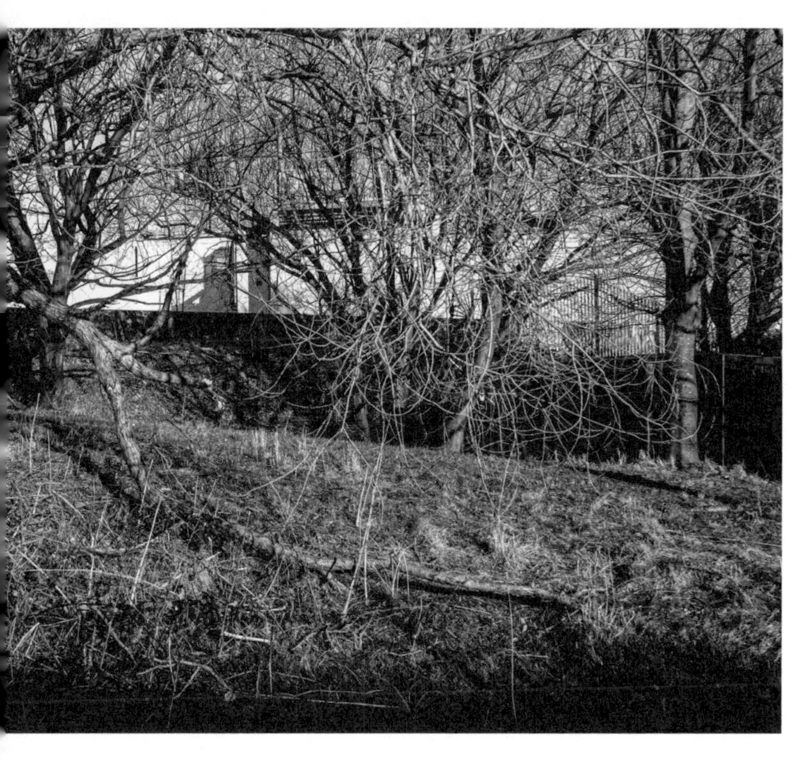

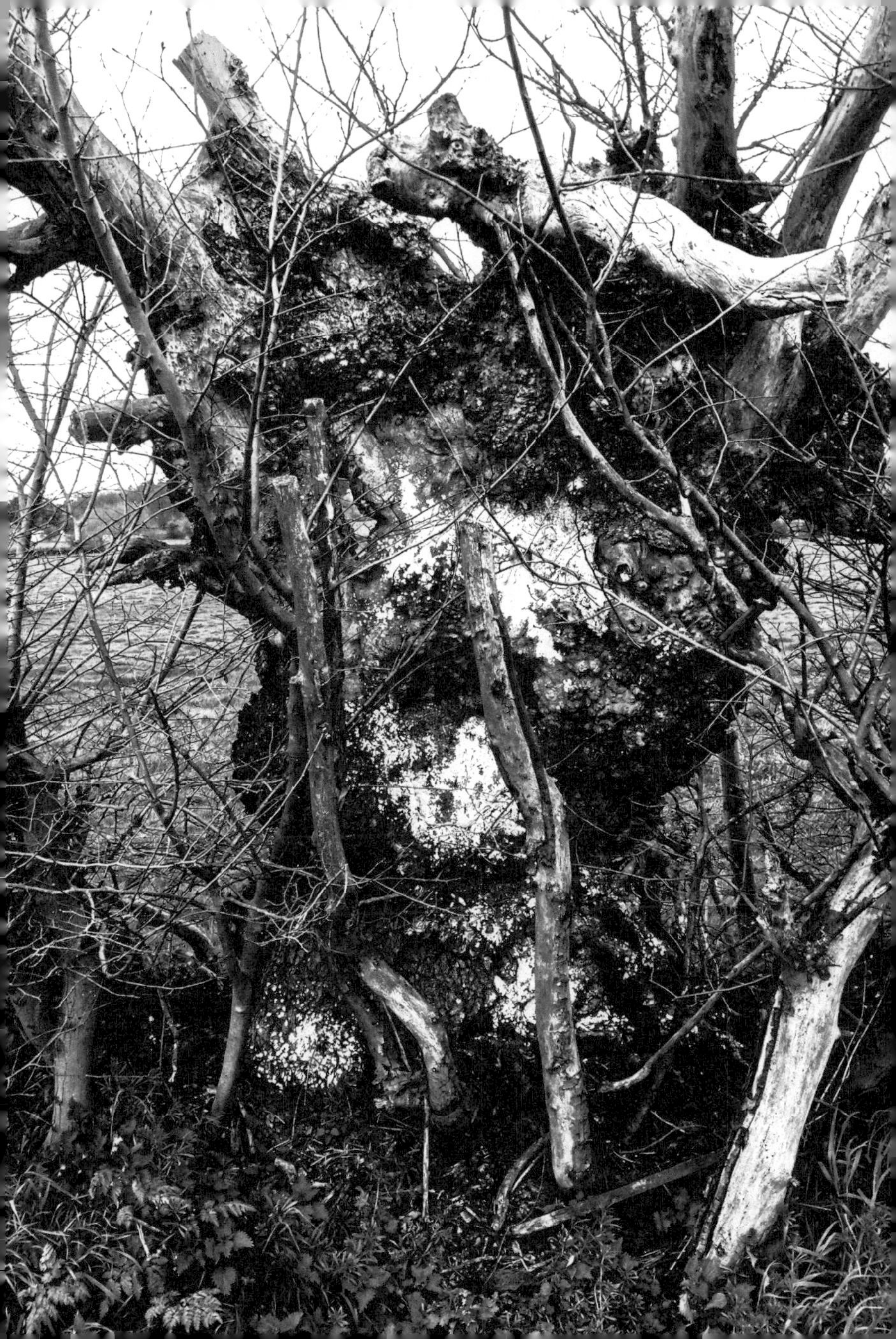

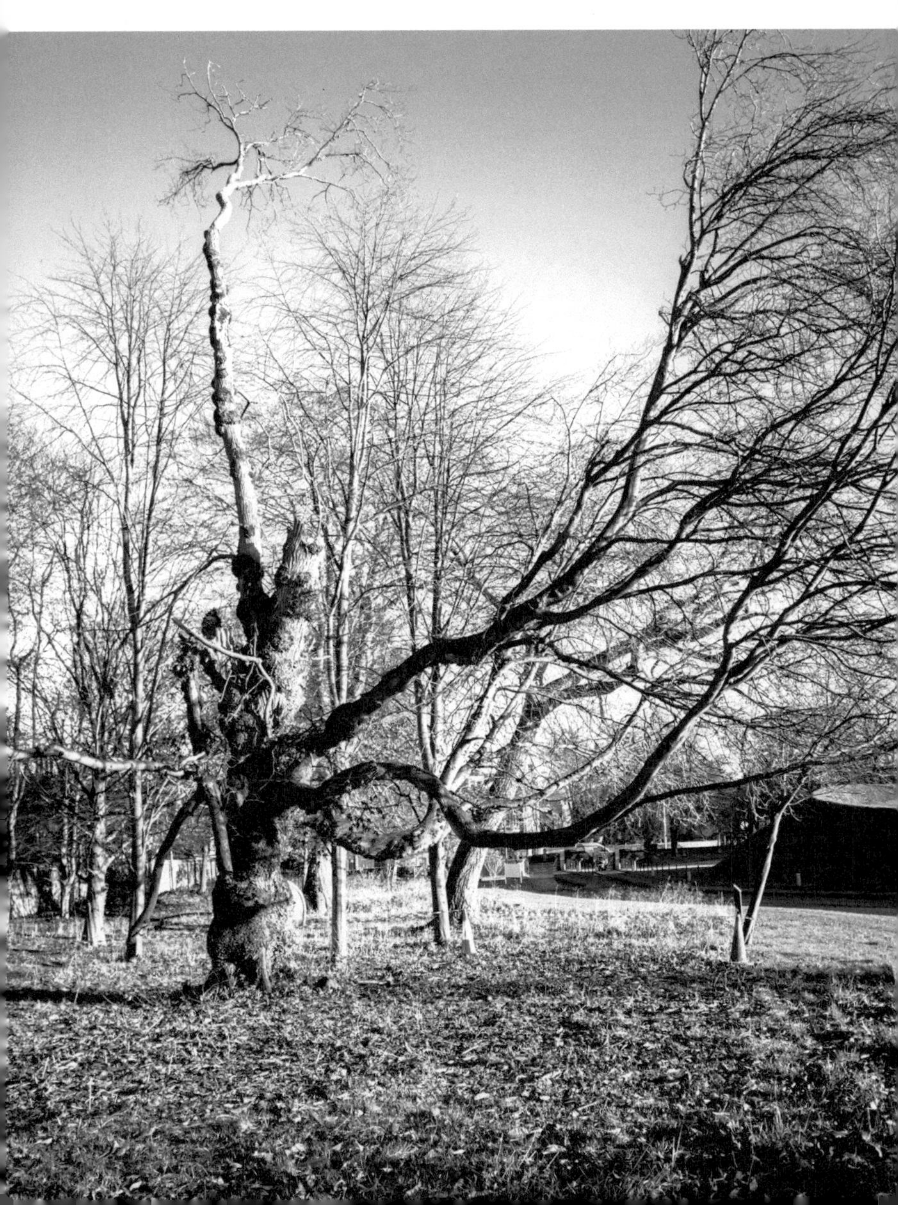

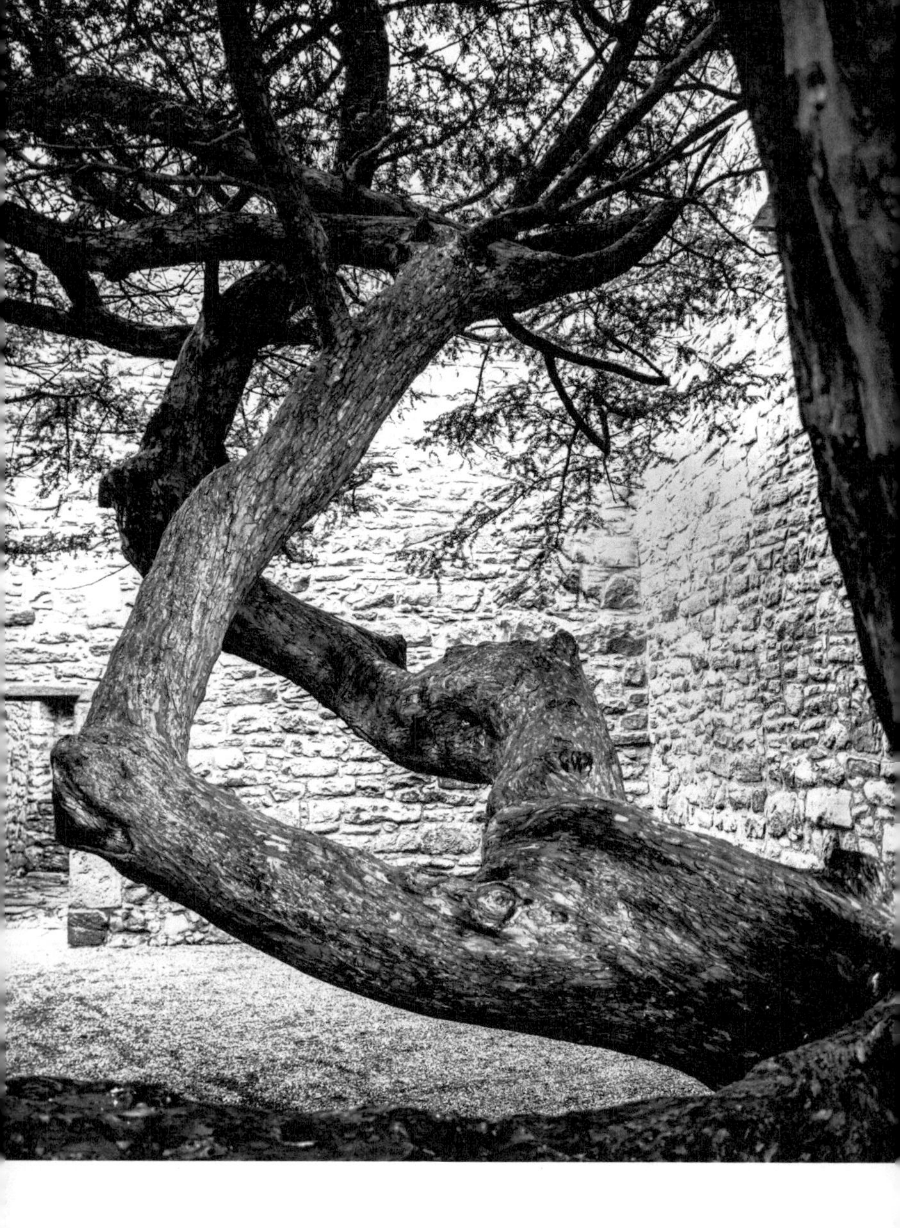

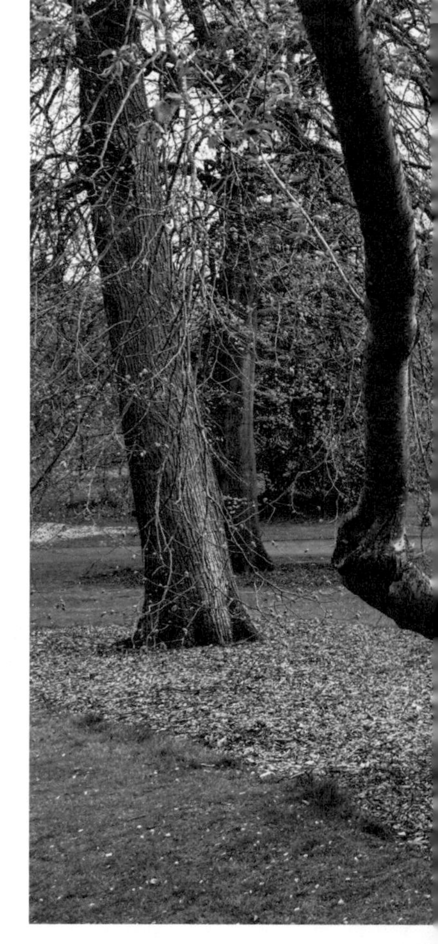

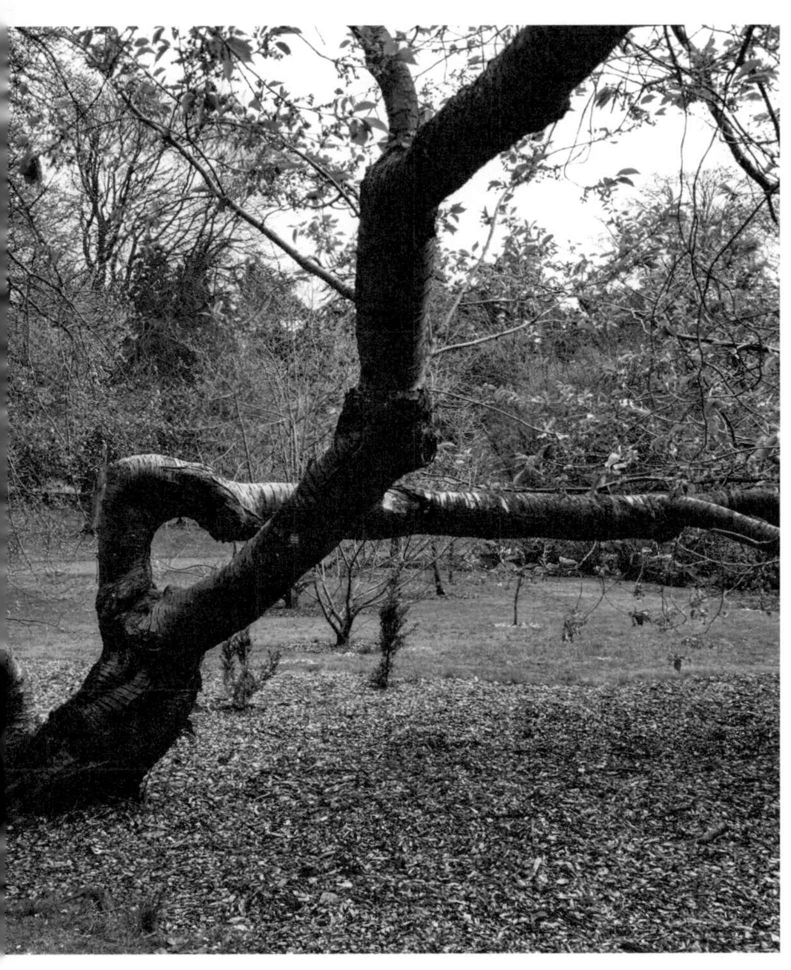

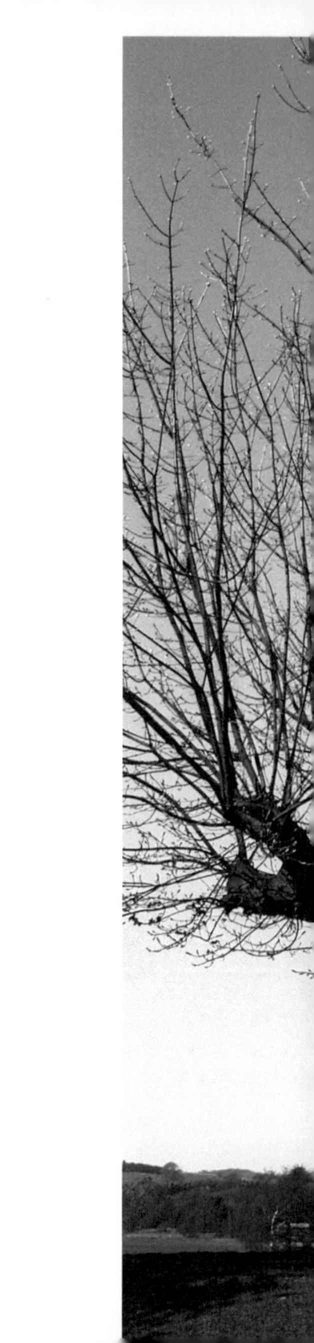

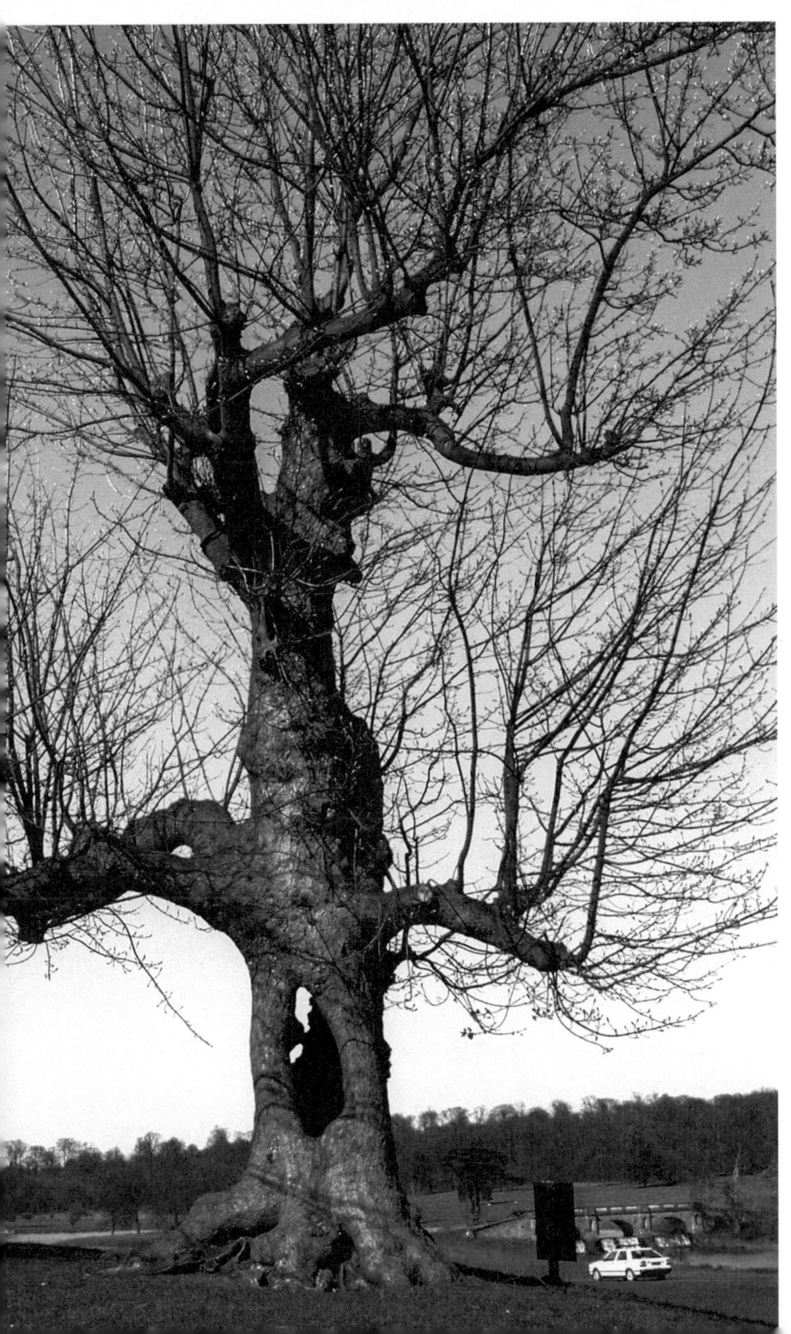

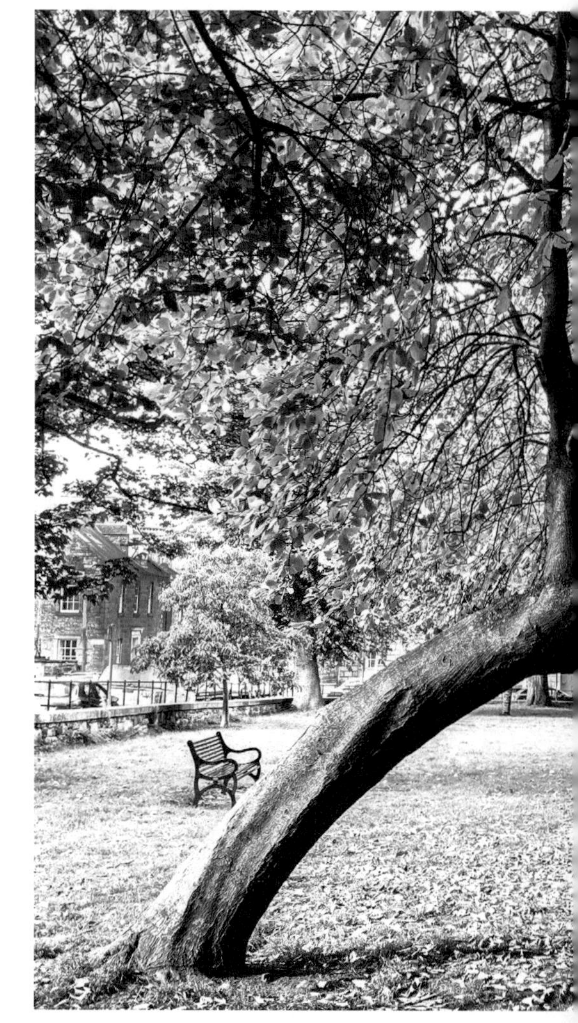

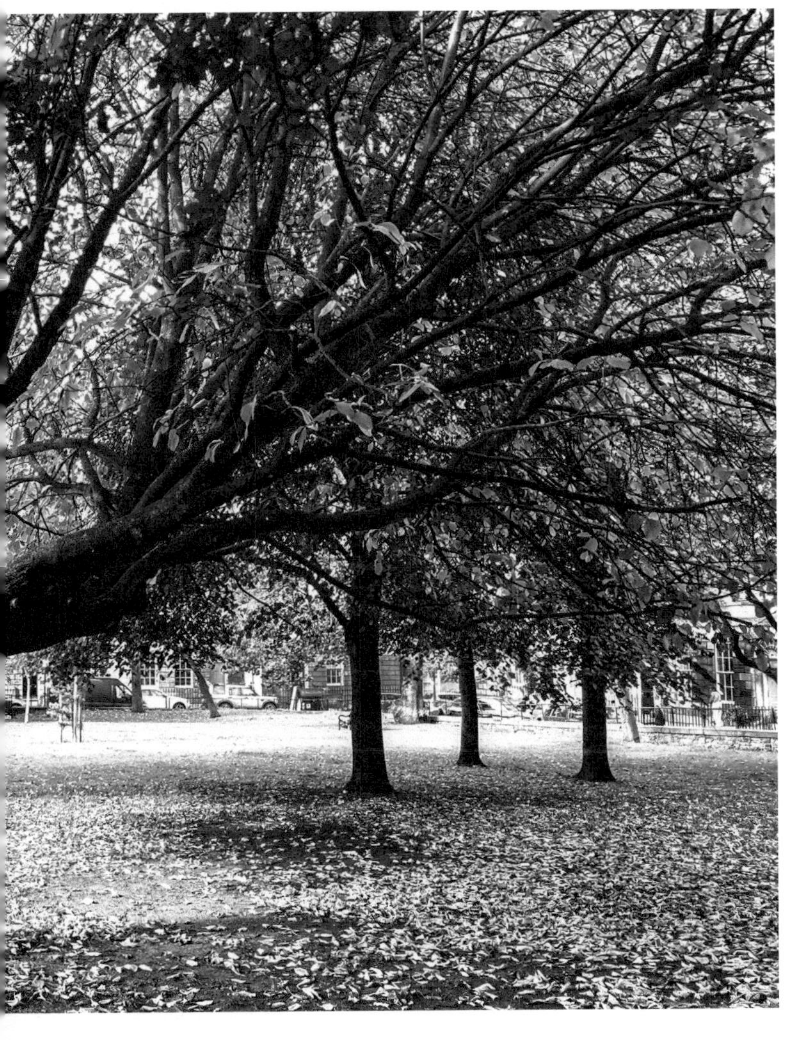

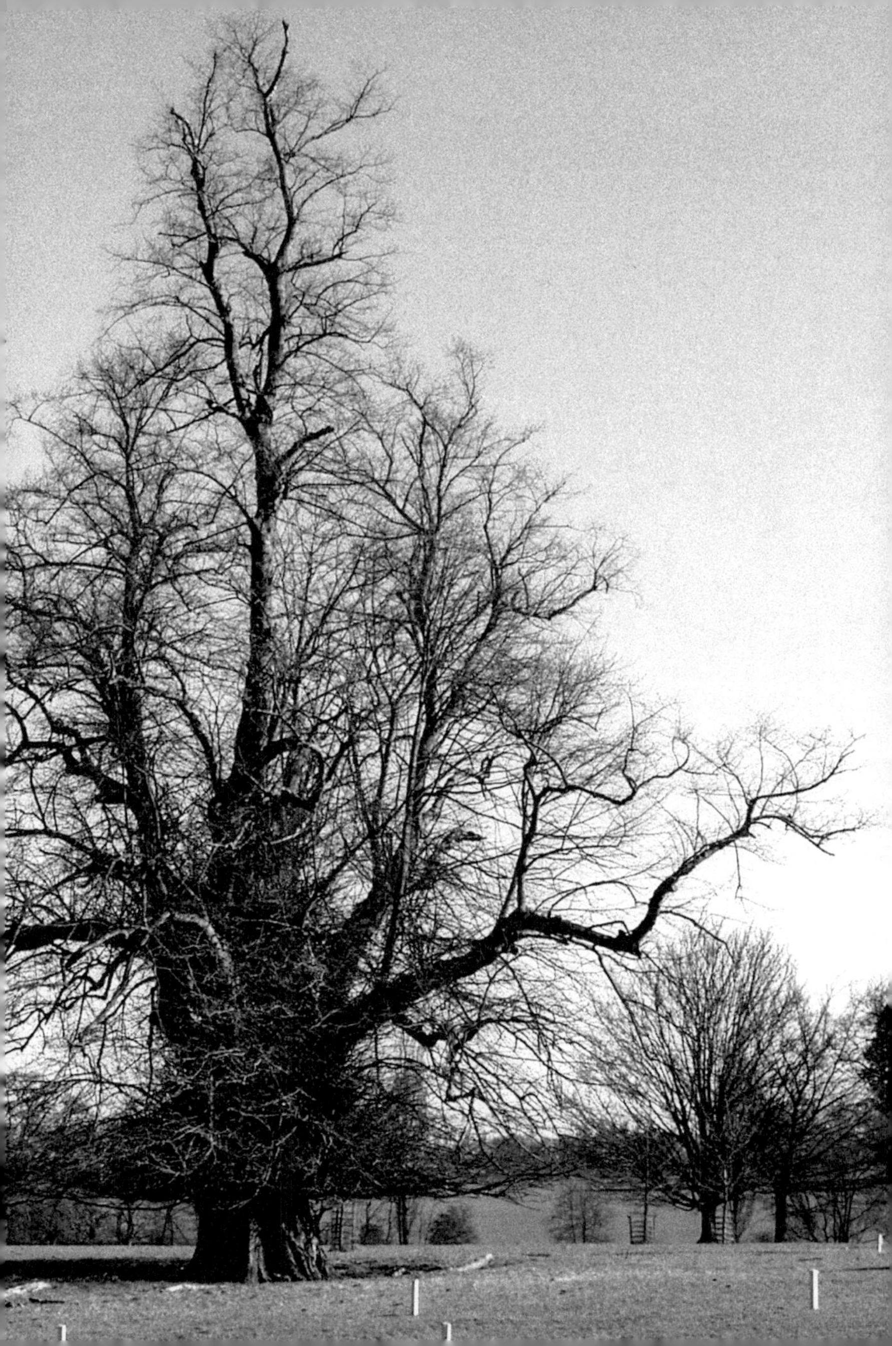

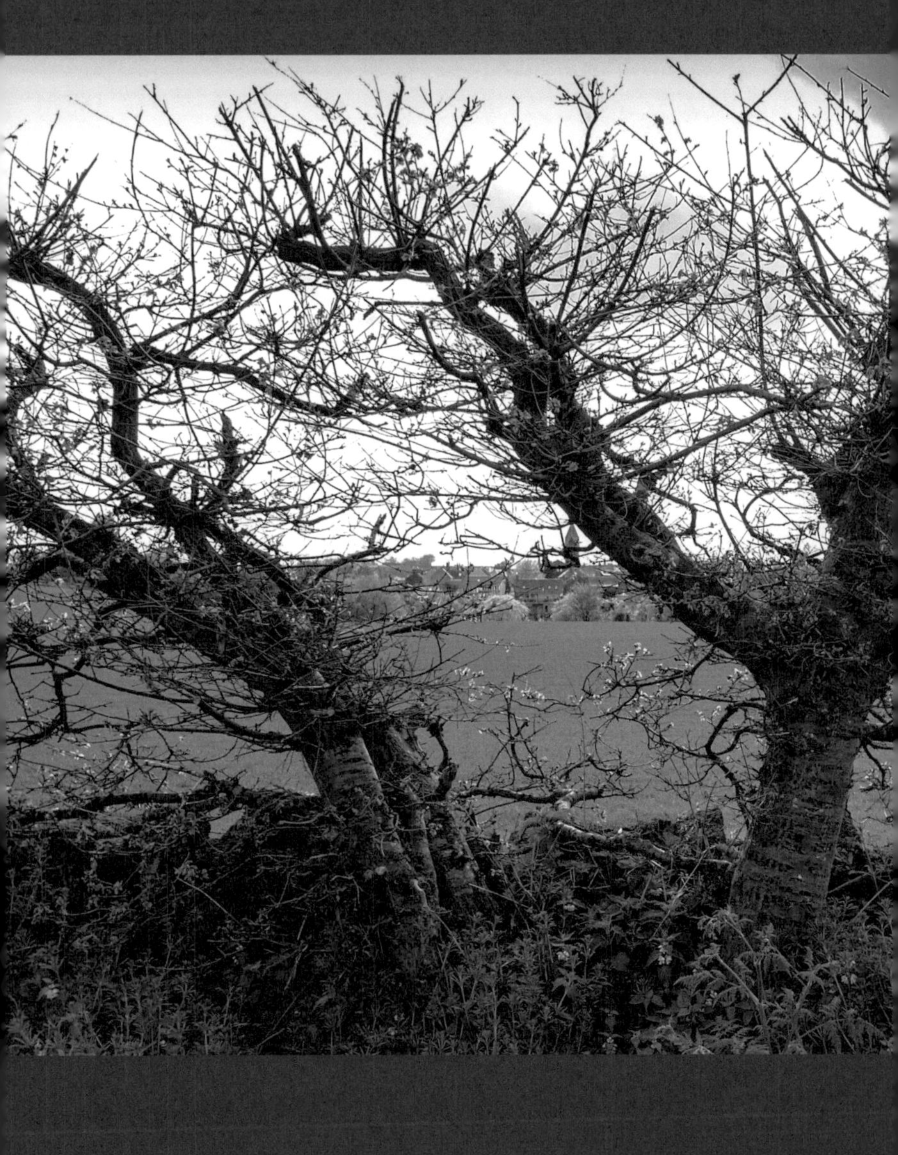

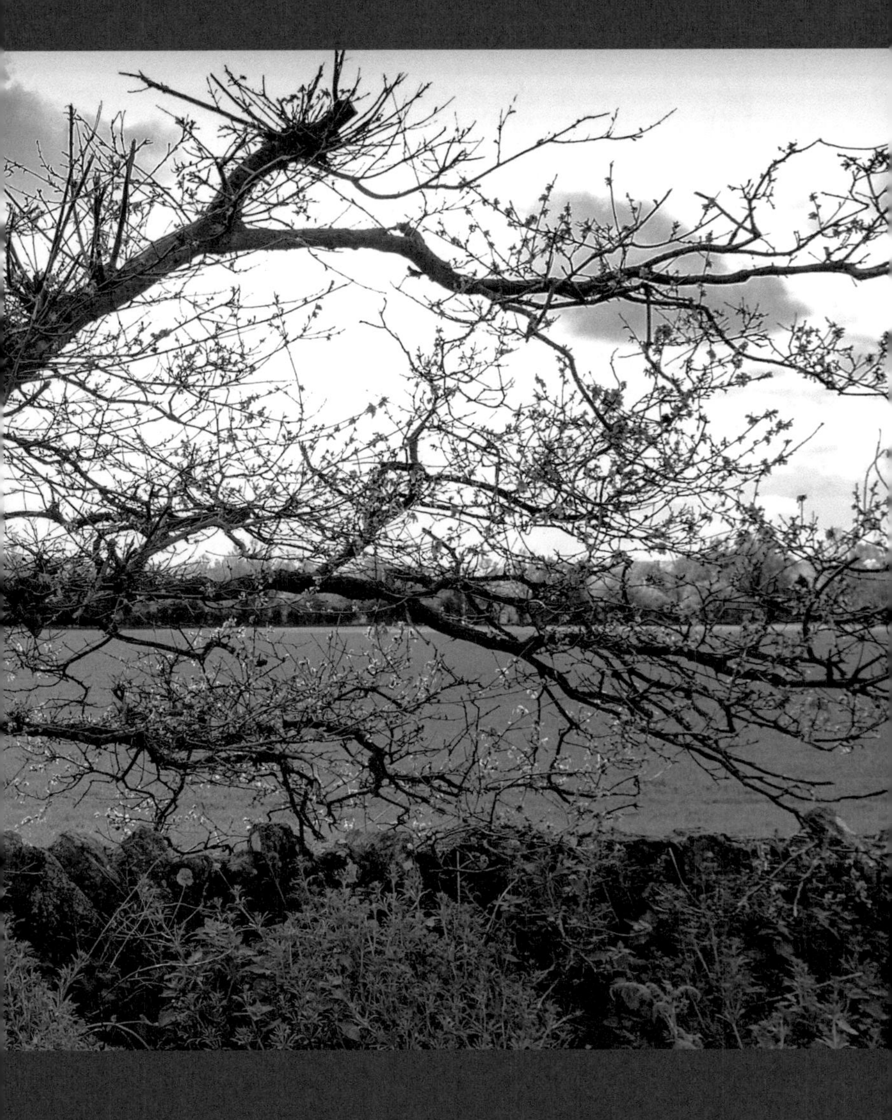

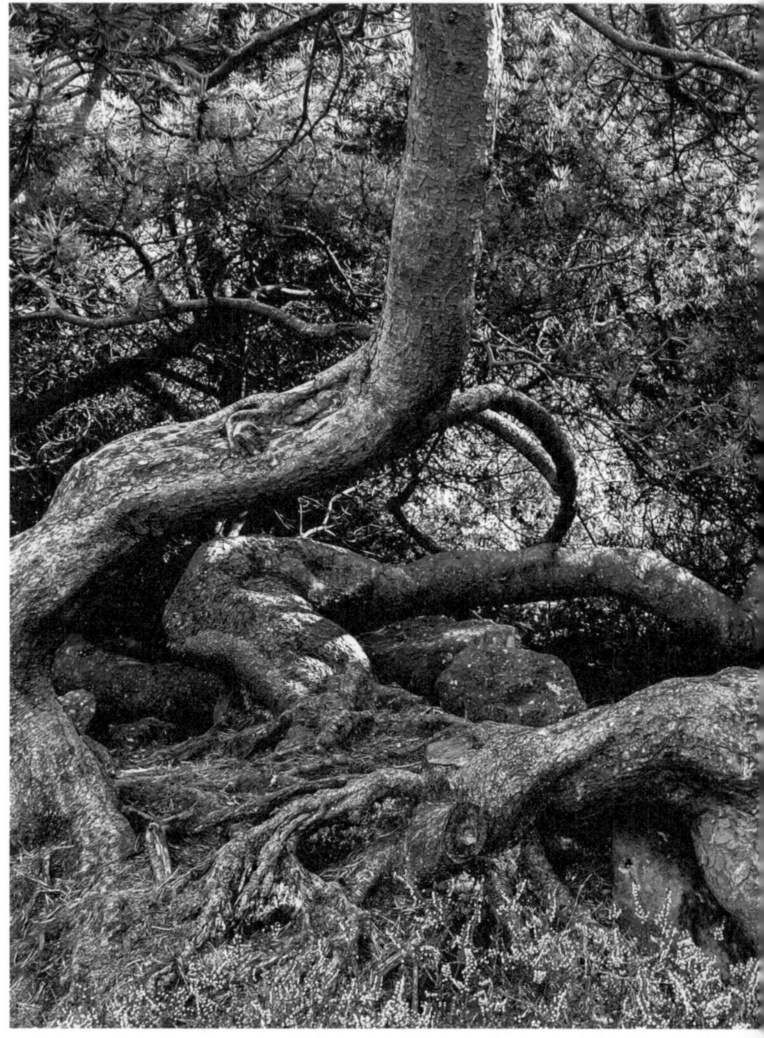